WEAM NAMOU

Chaldean Storyteller in Baghdad

Hermiz
Publishing Inc.

Library of Congress Control Number

2025927993

Published in the United States of Americaby:

Hermiz Publishing,Inc.

Sterling Heights,MI

10 9 8 7 6 5 4 3 2 1

First edition

ISBN: 978-1-945371-23-3

This book was professionally typeset on Reedsy.
Find out more at reedsy.com

For my parents,
Hermiz and Shamamta

What is remembered lives.

Contents

One

The Big Secret

Once upon a time, many years ago, a little Chaldean girl lived in the vibrant city of Baghdad, in a small concrete house. One day, a suitcase arrived at her door. It came from America, filled with gifts of toys and clothes. Inside was her very first doll, nearly as tall and wide as she was—a "mini-me" that she longed to touch. She wished to remove the clear plastic seal that covered her, and for a brief moment, she was able to admire the doll's silk dress and hair ribbons before someone tightly sealed the plastic again and placed the doll in a safe corner, waiting for the girl to play with it one day. "When we get to America," her family promised, "you can play with it all you want."

In that suitcase was also a short-sleeved red dress that she wore for Easter. Her family worried she would outgrow it before they reached America, as immigration petitions took years to process.

More important than the beauty of the doll and the dress was their origin. When guests arrived, the family suddenly discarded their unspoken rule about America. They proudly displayed their new toys and clothes, emphasizing that everything was from America. The little girl had her picture taken in the red dress, standing beside her two best friends.

That little girl was me, Weam. In Arabic, Weam is a unisex name meaning "harmony." As a Chaldean, I belong to the Neo-Babylonian community that still speaks the language we call Chaldean, which Westerners refer to as Aramaic—the language of Jesus.

Baghdad is the capital of Iraq. Its name means "Gift of God," which is derived from old Persian. The city was founded in 762 CE by the Abbasid caliph Al-Mansur, who built it as his new capital and formally named it *Madinat al-Salam*—the City of Peace. Yet the older name, Baghdad, endured, carried forward through centuries of history.

And Iraq, a land far away to many and unimaginably ancient, is layered with memory like a cake baked over millennia, each generation resting upon the last. Once called Mesopotamia, it holds biblical roots that reach back to the prophet Abraham, who came from Ur of the Chaldeans, from whom we trace our ancestry. This is the cradle of civilization, where writing was born, where the wheel turned for the first time, where sailboats cut across rivers, and where the world's first city-states rose from the earth.

Today, most people in Iraq are Muslim, but for a very long time the land has been home to many different peoples. Kurds, Turkmen, Yazidis, Mandeans, and families from other countries all lived side by side. Among them was a small community of Iraqi Christians who carefully passed down their faith, their language, and their traditions like precious heirlooms, worn smooth by many hands over time.

Our little house had a rooftop where, during the summer, people slept in the open air while sandstorms blanketed the streets. The neighborhood homes featured spacious yards and gardens surrounded by high walls or fences—not for security, as it was safe for people to leave their doors and windows unlocked, but mainly for privacy. Yet that word, privacy, felt as foreign to the natives of that land as French fries. The major streets were lined with palm trees, while others boasted olive, fig, pomegranate, apple, apricot, plum, lemon, and other local fruit trees that adorned the courtyards. They provided shade during the sweltering summer days and added a touch of greenery. Flower gardens dotted with grass faced the front of the house.

I lived with my parents, Mamma and Babba, who had twelve children, though not all of us grew up together. Seven were girls and five were boys. I was the eleventh child, the youngest girl, with my brother two years younger than me. Our family had one big dream—so big that it had to be kept a secret. It was the dream of moving to America, something I can share now, but we couldn't then.

In Baghdad, America was like a captivating perfume. It stirred emotions and transported people to another place and time, even into the cosmos. Each time the mailman arrived with a letter postmarked from the USA, my family's eyes sparkled with tears of love and dreams. Their lips curved into smiles, their shoulders lifted, and they seemed to stand a little taller. Their mood shifted as easily as turning a doorknob. It felt as if they had been handed a bundle of gold coins, not just a letter from my oldest brother, Basim.

But soon after their joy, fears crept in. The older siblings quickly reminded the younger ones not to mention the letter, our brother in America, or any intentions of leaving Iraq.

"If the Iraqi government suspects we're planning to flee, we'll be locked up here forever," they warned.

I wanted to ask, "Are we locked up? What are we running away from?" But I held my tongue, knowing that whoever I asked would simply lift a finger to their lips and say, "Shhhh."

As a little girl in Baghdad, my younger brother and I listened in awe as our sister, seven years older, shared stories about America, painting it as a magical place. She told us that everyone in America owned and rode horses. I guess cowboy movies were popular in Iraq.

"In America, one never runs out of eggs," she said. "Eggs are so plenty, people boil them by the dozens and play games with them where one person holds a hard-boiled egg and taps the egg of another person with his own egg, trying to break the other without breaking his own. They even crack eggs on each other's heads."

I am not sure whether she saw this on *The Three Stooges*, a show I learned about in later years, but my younger brother and I were in awe. Eggs in Iraq were a rare commodity, available to purchase in the *souk*, and only God and President Saddam Hussein knew when. It was not that Iraq had a shortage of eggs, or milk, or bananas, or tomatoes, or sugar, or chicken, or beef or whatever else was hard to find in the market. This was simply the Iraqi government's way of keeping its people "busy," or as Americans would say, "oppressed."

Back then, I hid the word "America" in my pocket, careful not to let anyone catch a whiff of it, while I went about my life, going to school and playing with friends. We had so much fun!

In the 1970s children owned the streets during the hours when they were not in school. We were like the train gate in control of traffic. When a car drove by, we scattered left and right to make way, and once the car passed, we resumed playing jump rope, hopscotch, tag, hide-and-go-seek, and the all-time favorite, marbles, where we drew a circle on the ground with a stick, placed all the marbles in the circle, then shot their smooth and brightly colored glass sphere to knock the other marbles out of the circle.

We did not worry about thieves or kidnappers because most mothers stayed at home and watched the children, theirs and the whole neighborhoods', as if they had binoculars implanted on all sides of their heads. We didn't have toys, board games, or electronic games. Most homes had a television and a radio, and some people had telephones too, though not us. Television programming started at 6 pm, opening with Quranic prayers, then children's shows, followed by regular family programming, and the news. By midnight, the screen would go dark and then the colored bars came on, followed by the pink noise and static-filled screen. In the summer, two additional hours of programming were added in the morning to get the kids out of their mother's hair. Our district was our amusement park. We didn't need waterslides, merry-go-rounds, Ferris wheels, roller coasters, cotton candy, popcorn, and lemonade. We just had a simple desire to be together and to be creative.

Summers in Iraq were so hot, people would say, "you can fry eggs under the sun." The adults would dismantle our beds and carry them along with the mattresses, pillows, bed sheets, and blankets to the rooftop, where they were set up in rows so we could sleep under an open sky. The rooftop was real entertainment. During broad daylight, we would go to the rooftop and watch the man in a white tank top smoke, his arms resting over the roofless wall; a woman hang bed sheets, pajamas, nightgowns, and men's tank tops and pants on a clothesline; our neighbor's older sister hold up a mirror in a well-lit corner as she plucked her eyebrows; a young student across the street who liked to pace back and forth while reading his book.

In the falling twilight, we would crawl out of our beds on the rooftops to chase after the moon that changed direction whenever we changed direction. We'd stand on top of the beds, raise our voice, and call out to our friends next door, asking them, "What are you doing?" Or we argued about who the moon was actually following, us or them, until our mothers would hush us up and scuttle us back to bed. Lovers had their own secret way of utilizing the rooftop, which we were then too young to learn the details of.

Every July 14, we watched the fireworks celebrating the 1958 revolution that took place in Iraq. It marked the overthrow of the Hashemite monarchy established by King Faisal in 1932 under the support of the British. One July 14, as we competed with the neighbors across our roof, we screamed so loud and jumped so hard that the bed broke and we fell to the ground. The neighbors laughed hysterically, and we got up, all red-faced.

The rooftop was very nice, except for when we were woken up first thing in the morning with a spoonful of flies in our mouths.

Life in Baghdad had its challenges, and as old woman used to say in Chaldean, "*Tshata krakhish, wu il titeh kbayig.*" It means "At one year he walks and at two years he crawls." This term was used when one works very hard but still regresses. Despite this, my family and I held on to our big secret dream: moving to America for a brighter future.

Standing with my two best friends, Maysa (white dress), Weam (red dress), and Niran (navy dress).

The 1955 Abboud building, designed by Chadirji, was Baghdad's very first high rise.

Two

Midwives

My mother's water broke while she was in the shower one winter day in December. She told my fifteen-year-old sister, Niran, to call the midwife, but we didn't have a phone. So, Niran rushed to a neighbor who did. Unfortunately, the midwife wasn't home, so Niran left a message with a family member and returned with the bad news. My mother urged her to try again.

On the way back, Niran encountered my great-uncle's wife, Hania, who was approaching with one of her seven sons. "I noticed your mother hasn't visited anyone for the past three days," Aunt Hania said. "Something told me to check up on her."

Since a phone call wasn't an option and letters were too formal and often went unread, people relied on their senses to communicate. Aunt Hania had a feeling that something significant was happening, and she was right.

Niran quickly explained the desperate situation. Aunt Hania didn't hesitate. She marched into our home, removed her abaya—a long black cloak worn for convenience—and did so with a swift and stoic demeanor, signaling the seriousness of the moment. "No need to get the midwife," she said. "I'll deliver the baby myself. Just bring hot water and rags."

Niran rushed to the kitchen while Aunt Hania went to my mother's side. As she ushered me into the world, she reassured my mother not to worry or be afraid. "If it's a boy, you can keep him. If it's a girl, I'll take her for my youngest son," she added, meaning when I grew up—her son was still in diapers at that time.

The midwife arrived just in time to cut the cord, but my birth was easy; my mother was in labor for hardly an hour. I was named Weam, a unisex name that means harmony, peace, and love, especially between friends or nations.

All my siblings were born at home except for my younger brother, who was born in a hospital. Home births were once the norm, and even my paternal aunt, Amto Hassina, was a midwife—the most renowned midwife of them all!

Aunt Hassina practiced in Fallujah, about forty miles from Baghdad. She was one of the few, if not the only, Christians in a city that dates back to Babylonian times. Fallujah was known for its important Jewish academies and later as the city of mosques due to its over 200 mosques.

Aunt Hassina lived alone with her son, Sabri, after her husband went missing in a war. Though they never found him, she stayed in Fallujah and, thanks to my father's support, became a nurse. People often knocked on her door in the middle of the night, calling, "Umm Sabri! So-and-so is in labor!"

In the Arab world, parents receive the honorary titles of abu (father of) and umm (mother of), followed by the name of their firstborn. My aunt would stumble out of bed, put on her abaya, and rush outside. The next day, families would arrive at her home with boxes of live chickens, fresh eggs, dried dates, and figs as tokens of gratitude, along with money, of course.

Aunt Hassina primarily delivered babies for the wives and daughters of sheikhs. While I don't remember her well, my siblings say she was the best among our paternal aunts, and "Everyone in Fallujah loved her."

"Aunt Hassina worked for decades among tribes who loved and respected her," one of my aunts would say. "She saved many lives, especially those of newborn girls. Long ago, in Fallujah, it was customary for fathers to bury newborn girls if they wished. Your aunt, being educated and compassionate, convinced them not to."

"How did she do that?" I asked.

"With an effective tongue, how else?"

"I mean, what did she say?"

"She used anecdotes from the Quran. Islam forbids such evil acts," she whispered, lightly tapping my hand. "It says that on Judgment Day, buried girls will rise from their graves and ask for what crime they were killed."

"Really?"

"Killing infant girls was an old custom in the Arab world. People were ignorant then and considered women less valuable than men," she continued. "Your Babba encouraged her to go to nursing school and supported her. Babba and his only brother, Dawood, were just as effective communicators as Aunt Hassina. They could play with words like chess pieces, building temples with them like architects and engineers. Many turned to your father for legal advice or representation in court."

"Why?"

"Why?" She laughed. "Because he was smart, honest, and didn't charge."

My mom (purple dress), her Uncle Zaya, his wife Hania—who delivered me—and their son in front.

Fallujah, where my aunt cared for mothers and families as a nurse and midwife.

Three

The Horrible Principal

I had walked to school that morning in my custom-made uniform, hair in braids tied with bright white imitation silk ribbons. The frosty grass crunched under my shoes, and the sounds of birds chirping hinted at the arrival of spring. Each click of my shoes echoed against the ancient stone, which once made Baghdad the wealthiest city in the world.

Before the bell rang, all the students lined up in the courtyard to watch the raising of the Iraqi flag and sing the national anthem.

My homeland, my homeland,

Glory and beauty, sublimity and splendor

Are in your hills, are in your hills.

Life and deliverance, pleasure and hope

Are in your air, are in your air.

Will I see you, will I see you?

Safely comforted and victoriously honored.

Will I see you in your eminence?

Reaching to the stars, reaching to the stars

My homeland, my homeland.

The principal then stood at the front and firmly said, "Two students did not show up to Saddam's Parade yesterday. When I read your name, come to the front."

I was one of the two students. I had skipped Saddam's Parade for a sleepover with my niece, who had come over the day before with her mother. We drank tea and enjoyed *tekhratha*, delicious meat and cheese pies. When she begged me to stay the night, I explained to my family what the teacher had said about the parade, "It's mandatory to attend." They didn't take it seriously, so I joined my niece instead.

Now, as I faced the principal, I felt the weight of my choice.

The principal called a sixth-grade girl. With her head bowed, her braid ribbons spread on each side like butterfly wings, the girl walked between the rows of students in school uniforms which resembled dominos ready to be toppled. She stood in front of the principal, who raised her ruler high. As it struck the girl, a sharp snapping sound echoed in the courtyard. She returned to her place with tears streaming down her face. I was next.

The principal called my name, and similarly to the girl before me, I walked between the lines of dominos, I mean students, to the front. Looking at the principal was frightful. She had a clenched jaw, piercing eyes with a scowl that looked like daggers, and tightened red lips that seemed twisted into a knot.

"Why didn't you come to the parade?" Her voice cut through the courtyard like a knife as I stood before her, heart racing.

Before I could answer, her hand shot up, and with a swift motion, she slapped my cheek with a force I had never felt before. Everything went black.

When I came to, I was in my classroom, surrounded by my teacher's warm smile and the concerned faces of my classmates. "You're lucky you didn't come to the parade," someone whispered. "It was so crowded, we couldn't see anything."

Baghdad was a center of learning and trade, home to the House of Wisdom. This important place helped translate works from Greek, Persian, Sanskrit, Chinese, and Syriac into Arabic and introduced the idea of library catalogs. When the Mongols invaded Iraq in 1258, they destroyed the House of Wisdom and all other libraries in Baghdad, marking a tragic moment in Iraq's history. Still, an Arabic proverb says, "If you haven't seen Baghdad, you have not seen the world." Yet for decades to come, this slap was what stood out in my memory.

At home, I kept the incident to myself. But my uncle's chatty daughter spilled the news. My mother was upset but didn't confront the principal; her husband was a Baathist, after all. *"Lakboogh satana id-awir ibathen,"* she would say—"We don't want the devil to enter our house." Speaking out could jeopardize our hopes of moving to America, away from the Baathists.

A Baathist was someone aligned with the ruling party. Speaking out against them could cost you your safety—and your future. We longed for a country with freedom and democracy.

It was the first time anyone had ever hit me. My parents didn't believe in spanking, perhaps because of George, my oldest brother who had died from croup as a toddler. My mother refused to talk about him.

On another day in science class, the teacher asked me a question. I stood there, tongue-tied, and was sent to the principal's office again. There, I faced her wrath once more. "Why didn't you answer the question?"

Before I could respond, she slapped me again. That was the second time someone laid a hand on me. My parents still didn't confront her, fearing for our future. I'm not sure whether my father ever knew of these incidents.

Schools in Iraq were serious business. If you failed one subject out of six, you had to repeat the whole year. Everyone focused on their studies, and teachers kept us in line. Daily, they checked our nails—clean and unpainted! Hair had to be neat in braids or ponytails.

Interestingly, there was no such thing as a bully among students. Kids cared for each other; no one made fun of another's appearance. If someone called another a name, they would face punishment. Calling someone *"duba hamisa"*, meaning chubby, was the worst. The teacher would investigate, and if found guilty, the offending student would get their hand slapped with a ruler. If they didn't extend their hands, they were hit on the legs.

The teachers and principals, though, could be bullies.

In some high schools, girls were let out half an hour before boys to avoid harassment.

My mother had never gone to school, so she couldn't help with our homework. My father tutored some of my siblings, and he tutored other peoples' children, but he had countless responsibilities, which I'll share in a separate chapter. I didn't need help, anyway; I was a good student who loved doing my homework. In the evenings, I laid on my stomach in front of the television, listening to "Open Sesame" or other shows, even the news, while I tackled math and other subjects.

My school supplies included a notebook with flowery designs where I wrote my name, school, teacher, class, and year; an eraser that smelled sweet as perfume; a flowery pencil; and chalk. But beneath the surface of my school life, fear and uncertainty loomed. Every snap of the ruler and harsh word from the principal reminded me of how fragile our lives were under the Baath control.

That night, as I lay in bed, I clutched my notebook and dreamed of a safe future.

In our sturdy, thick-brick home, my family dared not utter Saddam's name—not even in the dead of night, when the country lay silent and the streets outside seemed deserted. The fear was intense, like the heavy air before a storm. I often wondered: were there ghosts in the room, listening? What would happen if they reported our whispered fears to him? *"Gudaani itta nethyatha,"* the elders would caution in Chaldean. "The walls have ears." Though I had never met this Saddam, his name cast a shadow over us, as if he were a ghost haunting every corner of our lives.

I closed my eyes, hoping that tomorrow would bring new chances and a little more freedom.

My sister Basima and her daughter Ban, at whose home I had a sleepover.

Me with my friends, years before everything changed.

Iranian Prime Minister Amir-Abbas Hoveyda during a visit to Iraq, hosted by Saddam Hussein, 1975.

Four

Ghosts

One night, my oldest sister Basima joined a group of relatives in our living room for tea. The scent of cardamom and mint mingled with the sound of their laughter. Basima had an aura about her, her striking features reminiscent of Souad Husni, the famous Egyptian actress. People often stopped her in the streets, asking if she was a movie star, especially when she wore her oversized sunglasses. But tonight, it wasn't her beauty that captivated us—it was the stories that were shared.

They chatted about ghosts, neglecting to notice the children sitting around them on the floor. I was scared by what I had heard.

One story had to do with our neighbor Fatin who, one night, was on her rooftop, enjoying the cool evening breeze. Suddenly, a shadowy figure startled her, sending her screaming into the night. We rushed to our balcony, watching as men hurried to her aid. Rumors spread quickly—some claimed she had leaped from the roof in fright, others insisted she had mistaken a harmless shadow for a ghost. Whispers even suggested it was a thief who had jumped off the roof, terrified of being caught.

The story grew with each retelling, the details becoming more elaborate and dramatic. The conversation then spiraled into tales of ghosts. One woman recounted a chilling story. A young lady stood nervously at a busy intersection in the pouring rain, drenched and waiting to cross. A man noticed her, took off his coat, draped it over her shoulders, and walked her home. The next day, he returned to ask for her hand in marriage. But when he arrived, her family told him he had the wrong house. He insisted it was the right one and gave them her name, only to learn their daughter had died years ago. In disbelief, they took him to the cemetery, where they found his coat draped over her grave.

"Only small-minded people believe in ghosts," someone scoffed.

Basima leaned forward, her dark eyes sparkling like stars. "That's not true! My aunts believe in them, and they are anything but small-minded."

"They didn't believe in ghosts; they believed in *fatah al fal*," another sister interjected, referring to fortune tellers. This sparked a flurry of laughter and stories about their family's superstitions.

Basima recounted a tale about our paternal aunts, who often visited fortune tellers to uncover the thief stealing their gold jewelry. Unbeknownst to them, the culprit was their own nephew. Stifling her laughter, Basima described how the fortune teller accused a series of strangers, all while the real thief sat among them, pretending innocence. 'Can you believe they even brought him along to help catch the thief?' she exclaimed. The room erupted with laughter, the irony too outrageous to ignore."

As the conversation shifted, the women began to speak of jinn—mysterious spirits from ancient Arabian myths, made of smokeless fire and capable of taking on any form. Some were said to be benevolent, but others were malevolent, their intentions unclear. "Be careful, or a jinn might visit you at night," one relative joked, though her tone carried an edge. My heart raced as I listened, the shadows in the room growing longer.

In Arabic folklore, someone said, sleep paralysis happened when a jinn pressed down on a person, attempting to possess them. The thought sent a chill through me.

"This reminds me of Tantal," one of the women said, her voice dropping to a conspiratorial whisper.

"Tantal?" Basima asked, raising an eyebrow.

"Yes," the woman replied. "He's no jinn, but he's just as frightening. They say he roams the marshes at night, guarding treasures buried beneath the mud. If a child wanders too far from home, Tantal will snatch them up before they even realize what's happening."

Another woman chimed in, nodding. "He's not just after children. Tantal is a trickster. If you're brave and clever, you might convince him to tell you a secret or even show you where the treasure is. But if you're weak or scared..." She trailed off, letting the silence linger.

Basima smirked, always the skeptic. "So, what happens to the ones who aren't brave enough?"

"They say he drags them into the marshes, where they vanish without a trace," the first woman replied matter-of-factly. "But, of course, that's just what they tell children to keep them from running off."

The group laughed, though uneasily, as if trying to convince themselves it was only a story. But the mention of Tantal stuck with me, weaving into my thoughts alongside the tales of jinn.

That night, I tossed and turned, unable to shake the unease that had settled over me from all this talk about ghosts.

The following morning, I awoke to a man's face just inches from mine—a ghostly figure, pale as snow, gliding over me like an open palm closing a dead person's eyes. His features were sharp, handsome even, but a darkness surrounded him, paralyzing my ability to scream or move. Frozen, my mind raced with all the stories I had heard. Was this a jinn?

After dressing for school, I stepped into the backyard, the sun warming my face, only to spot that same face floating in midair, its presence suffocating. It appeared again on my walk to school, visiting me repeatedly before it finally faded away.

Years later, in America, the same face returned. This time, I screamed so loud that I woke the entire house. My family rushed in, discovering it was just a nightmare, and soon returned to sleep. Only later did I realize whose face I had seen: Saddam's.

My sisters Basima and Kheloon in our backyard, long before the ghost stories took shape.

Women gathered.

Five

Living in a Muslim Country

"Allah is the greatest. I bear witness that there is none worthier of worship except Allah."

The *muezzin's* voice in the nearby mosque poetically chanting the Quran woke up the city of Baghdad. The adhan was a sound I had grown up with, a reminder of the world around us. Though we were Christian, the call to prayer was as much a part of our daily life as the church bells we heard on Sundays. The smell of cardamom tea and fried eggs and onions, the breakfast my mother was cooking, reached the rooftop as the adhan came through loudspeakers that seemed to fill the entire world. The call was scheduled five times per day, and hearing it, I entered a dreamy, drowsy state, even when I was already drowsy.

We loved many of our neighbors, and many neighbors loved us in return, but some considered us untrustworthy infidels and nonbelievers, unfit for friendship. My mom often reminded us, "There are good and bad people everywhere," a lesson she held close even when she learned

26

that the kind gardener, whom she had welcomed into our home and provided daily lunches, had been throwing the meals in the bushes.

It was a Friday morning, and in Muslim countries, Fridays marked a holy day and the weekly day of congregational prayer at the mosque. Schools closed, so our week kicked off on Saturday and ended on Thursday.

One day, I got up in my *dishdasha*, nightie, and to the sound of cooing doves, went downstairs to the living room. My older sisters were busily spreading a bed sheet over the floor and arranging the breakfast dishes and Iraqi teacups called *istikan*, a word the British used to describe the container used to serve tea, so *East Tea Can*.

There were a lot of us to feed, and much work to be done. My mother sent me on a mission: "Go get some fresh bread from the bakery."

Without changing out of my nightie, I headed out. Back then, it wasn't unusual to see people still in their nightclothes, especially on Fridays when everyone was lounging at home.

Arriving at the bakery, I was hit by the warm, inviting aroma of baked bread wafting through the air. My eyes widened as I gazed at the tub where the freshly baked loaves tumbled out. But as I stepped closer, a wave of adults surged forward, arms reaching and hands grabbing. I stood there, small and invisible, waiting for my turn that never seemed to come. Time ticked by, and frustration bubbled inside me until one of my sisters appeared, searching for me.

"What happened?" she asked, eyebrows knitted in concern.

I sighed, "No one is giving me a chance to get the bread."

She stared at me compassionately. Taking my hand as we walked home, she shared stories about our beloved tandoor ovens, how they'd been baking our bread for over 5,000 years. She told me about women waking before dawn to bake, and children gathering around to learn the craft. "You know," she said, "boys used to sneak up and steal food from the ovens all the time."

"Did they ever get caught?" I asked.

"Oh yes! They'd get caught and shooed away and come the next day for more!"

We were both laughing by the time we got home. Someone else was sent for the bread.

Later that month, as Christmas approached, my best friend Niran and her family came to the door to wish us a Merry Christmas. Her mother, dressed in a long, flowing abaya, handed my mother a tray of sweets. "We hope you have a blessed holiday," she said warmly.

Niran and I ran off to play, our laughter echoing through the street as we raced to her house and back. Her family didn't celebrate Christmas, but they always treated our holiday with respect, just as we did theirs. Every year during Eid al-Fitr, my mother and I would rush to Niran's house to wish her family *Eid Mubarak* and admire her new clothes, which her mother had sewn by hand.

At home, our Christmas celebrations were simple. There were no glittering trees or piles of presents like those at my relatives' homes, but there was always laughter, *kleicha* (Iraqi cookies), and a special food that Iraqis of all faiths feasted on during special occasions—*pacha*, a hearty dish made from all parts of lamb, like the tripe, trotters, the head, brain, tongue, and even eyes! Watching my mother prepare pacha was an event in itself, from stitching the tripe pockets to meticulously adding the spices. But for me, the eyeballs staring back from the bowl were simply too much. While the adults divided my portion with laughter, I decided that some traditions were better appreciated from a distance—preferably one where the food couldn't look back at me.

We did not find the spirit of the season in elaborate decorations or lavish meals. It was in the laughter we shared, *the kleicha* we baked, and the quiet joy of being together. I was content, blissfully unaware that anything might be missing.

That is, until my sister said it.

"Santa didn't come this year," she told me one evening, her voice light and cheerful, as though she were sharing a harmless piece of news. "There must have been a terrible snowstorm."

Her words landed like gum on the bottom of my shoe—sticking to my mind and refusing to let go. I hadn't even realized Santa was supposed to come to our house. Until that moment, I hadn't been waiting for him, hadn't noticed his absence. But now, the absence was real.

Why didn't Santa come to our house?

I asked another sister about it, my voice small and uncertain. She smiled and said, "Oh, he'll be visiting us once we're in America."

I believed her. Everything seemed to be waiting for us there.

My sisters Khelood and Basima with Basim and their children at Christmas.

Domes of Al-Hayder Khana mosque, Baghdad, 1932.

St. Joseph Cathedral in Baghdad.

Six

Babba the Bonesetter

My father, Hermiz, knelt beside a man who sat on the couch, gently observing his leg while the man groaned in agony. My mother, Shamamta, carried a tub of warm water as she entered the living room, the steam curling around her like a shawl. She set the tub next to my father with care and placed towels nearby. Then she brought out a bumpy, delicious-smelling bar of olive-green soap, marked with Arabic inscriptions.

I sat on the floor in my nightie, watching Babba's hands move like they had a secret language of their own. The man's groans filled the room, but Babba's face stayed calm, his touch firm but careful. I couldn't look away, wondering how he knew what to do, as if his hands could see what the rest of us couldn't.

My father wore many hats in Baghdad. He was the head of the accounting department at Baghdad Railway Station, his desk stacked with ledgers and receipts. He worked as a translator, bridging Arabic and English for businessmen and officials. But his night role set him

33

apart—he was a bonesetter, a medicine man whose hands read injuries like a book. People came to our door with broken bones, dislocations, and torn ligaments, choosing his methods over hospital visits. He sent critical cases to doctors, but many found healing under his care alone.

One night, a rich man knocked on our door. He leaned on a cane, his face drawn with pain that Baghdad's doctors couldn't cure. He'd heard stories of my father's gift. After three sessions, my father set a date to check his progress, but the man didn't show up. Months later, they crossed paths. When my father asked about the missed appointment, the man gripped his hands.

"I never needed another treatment," he said. "Your touch healed me." My father smiled, but his voice stayed humble. "Thank God for that," he said.

Between healing bones and solving family legal troubles, Babba's life brimmed with purpose. He taught students in our home each evening and even helped his nephew prove his innocence when accused of theft by a large company. He dug through their ledgers until he found the error that cleared his nephew's name.

Yet, for all his talents, my father carried an unfulfilled dream: he had yearned to be a doctor, a calling that seemed to flow naturally in his veins, passed down through generations of healers—my grandfather, my aunts, my great-grandmother, and countless others whose names history has forgotten. He carried that dream with him into Baghdad College High School, one of the most respected schools in the country. Only a small number of boys were accepted each year, and my father was one of them. He was still a boy who wanted to heal people, who believed learning could open doors no one else could see.

The school had been founded by American Jesuit priests, and it felt different from anywhere else in Baghdad. The classrooms were plain, the floors uneven, and when dust storms swept in, the air turned thick and gritty. But the library—the *library*—was something else entirely.

To my father, it was a treasure chest. Shelves upon shelves of books waited for him, and for the first time in his life, he was allowed to take any book home, free of charge. He read at night until his eyes ached, carrying whole worlds back with him in his hands.

Baghdad College taught its students to think deeply, work carefully, and serve others. Though my father would not become a doctor, the discipline and love of learning he found there shaped the rest of his life. Numbers became his language, and service his calling.

He lived that calling quietly, in our living room, night after night.

Tonight's patient rose carefully, testing his newly wrapped leg bound in torn bedsheets. Another man helped him hobble to the door. As he left, the scent of Mother's cooking drifted in—sautéed beef with tomatoes and the sharp note of arak. These evening aromas filled our home, mixing with news broadcasts as my brother and I leaned over our homework.

Baghdad College, where Babba studied, pictured with Jesuit priests in front.

Baghdad College, established in 1932.

Seven

Babba's Baghdad

One, two, three, four... one, two, three, four. Babba left the house with purpose, as he did every morning, and headed toward Baghdad Railway Station to begin his important job.

Being the head of the accounting department was no small thing. In Iraq, there were jobs Christians were simply not meant to have. A Christian could not rule over Muslims in government offices or courts. Becoming a judge was out of reach. So were many leadership posts.

But numbers were different. Numbers, I guess, did not care what religion you were. And honestly, when it came to numbers, Babba was the smartest of them all. In the end, they had no choice.

One, two, three four... one, two, three, four. He passed the tea kettle makers, the yogurt and cheese sellers, and the chefs who shouted over one another, selling shish kebabs and shawarma that hissed on open grills—though maybe the right word for them was cooks or grill masters, not chefs. Dates shone dark and sticky in wooden crates. Tea glasses clinked. Red double-decker buses groaned past, tall and proud, their engines coughing dust into the air. Baghdad moved, and Babba moved with it, moving quickly now through the crowd and noisy traffic.

He arrived to the Baghdad Railway Station. Its turquoise dome caught the sun, and its twin clock towers never agreed on the time. One told time in Arabic numbers, the other in Roman numerals.

Inside, everything echoed. Shoes on marble. Voices calling destinations. Trains leaving for Basra, Mosul, and places that sounded impossibly far away—Jerusalem, London. One of his colleagues came up to him, looking nervous. "Abu Basim," he said. "The boss wants to see you."

Babba walked to the boss' office. His boss didn't even offer him a seat. He simply told him with utmost hatred, "Hermiz, you're being transferred to Samawa."

"Samawa?" my father asked. "That's some three hours away by train."

"Yes, and that's where you're being transferred."

My father was shocked, but he did not argue. He left, not sure how or why this happened. A kind man who liked Babba said to him, "They heard what you said about the Baath Party."

Babba did not join the Baath Party. He did not believe in it. He believed a man should not have to wear a badge to prove his loyalty, and he never pretended otherwise. He said this openly, the way he said most things, even when silence would have been safer. We were Christian too, and that alone was enough to count against us. At work, that honesty followed him. His boss was a Baathist.

When he left work that day, Babba stood and watched the platforms, his hands folded behind his back, thinking of the British men who had come from far away to build something meant to last. He bought from the market a bag of small green apples, and brought them home to us in a brown paper bag. My brother and I tied strings to their stems and spun them like toys. Babba watched us quietly.

"Come here," he said, gesturing for us to come sit beside him. We did.

"I want to tell you about the Baghdad Central State," he said, "the Crown Jewel of Baghdad."

"A jewel?" my brother asked. "Like in a treasure chest?"

Babba smiled. "Yes," he said. "Exactly like that."

He told us it was built by the British in the early 1950s and designed by a Scottish architect named J. M. Wilson.

"Who are the British?" my brother asked.

"That's a long story," he said. "They came from far away and ruled this land for a while.

"Before 1921, it was called Mesopotamia," Babba said. "It means *the land between two rivers*. That's where we are."

Then there were the clocks.

"When they chime," Babba said, "they sound like Big Ben."

"Who is Big Ben?" my brother asked.

He laughed, a laugh that took a while to die down. We waited.

"Imagine a super tall, fancy clock tower in London that rings a giant bell," he said. "The bell is so huge, as heavy as a school bus, that they gave it a name, Big Ben."

"A bell with its own name," I said in awe.

"Yes, and its bong has a voice of its own," he said. "The one that rings inside Baghdad's station, when it goes bong!, it's as if a piece of London had wandered into the Tigris Valley and decided to stay."

"Stay forever," my brother said.

At its busiest, Babba told us, the station had been a world of its own. It printed its own tickets. It had a bank. A restaurant where people dressed well and lingered over their meals. The printing press clacked all day long, keeping time with the arrivals and departures.

"A city inside the city," Babba said, his facial expression changing from pride to sadness as he picked up his istikan and had a sip of tea. He seemed far in thought.

40

Babba was proud of the Railway Station and the future it once promised. Then the promises began to disappear.

Al Sikak meant *The Tracks*. It was a neighborhood built for the men who worked on the railway—engineers, clerks, men like Babba. In those years, the railway mattered. Trains moved people and goods across the country, and the men who kept them running were respected.

The houses were solid and close to the station. Diplomats lived nearby. So did important officials. From Al Sikak, you could reach Al Karkh in minutes, and beyond it the palaces where presidents worked. The Republican Palace was rising then, and the neighborhood felt close to the future Baghdad imagined for itself.

The houses belonged to the government. Electricity was steady. Water ran clean. The streets were calm. Children played outside without being called in early. Now Babba had to live far away. Every week, sometimes every other week, he came home by train. He arrived with the same straight back, the same steady walk, as if nothing had been taken from him. But something had. Still, he found places where the world loosened its grip.

The coffeehouse was one of them.

Inside, smoke curled like lazy ghosts. Dominoes cracked sharply against wooden tables. Men argued, laughed, leaned back in their chairs as if time belonged to them. Here, Babba was no longer Hermiz. Here, he was the King of Dominos.

One evening, my mother sent my brother to fetch him. The boy he spoke to stood awkwardly in the doorway and said, "I don't know anyone named Hermiz."

"What do you mean?" my brother said. "He comes here all the time. Everyone knows him."

The boy asked the others. No one knew Hermiz.

"Abu Basim," my brother tried. "He's also known as Abu Basim."

That didn't help. They talked among themselves, puzzled, until one man suddenly laughed.

"Oh," he said. "You mean the King of Dominos. Why didn't you say so?"

Another man pointed. "Yes. The King."

My brother stood there, stunned. He hadn't known his father had another name.

"Next time," the man said kindly, "ask for the King, and everyone will know who you mean."

They fetched Babba.

My Babba—the accountant, the King of Dominos, the healer—like every man before him and since, yearned for freedom. Beyond caring for his family, that was his deepest desire.

Babba at his desk, head of the accounting department at the railway station.

Baghdad Railway Station, 1976.

Eight

Mamma Goes to School

My mother wore her abaya, grabbed her pencil and notebook, and headed out the door.

"Make sure you turn off the curry stew in half-an-hour," she instructed one of my older sisters while instructing the other to make sure the little ones were fed, which would be me and my younger brother, for this one to sweep and mop afterward, and so on and so forth, before she turned the door knob, opened the door, and left the house.

At age forty-five, she was going to school. For the first time. Not by choice, but by law. In 1978, the government decided my mother needed an education. Well, they didn't make that law just for her. Every illiterate Iraqi between fifteen and forty-five was required to attend literacy classes. Those who refused would pay a fine or spend a week in jail.

Classes were held in the evenings, after children had gone home and the men had finished their workdays. My mother walked into a classroom and paused. The desks were small. The chairs were worse.

44

Adults sat carefully, as if the furniture might report them.

A teacher smiled too brightly."Please," she said, pointing. "Sit."

My mother lowered herself into the chair, knees angled outward, dignity intact.

They began with letters.

"This is *alif*," the teacher said, writing it on the board.

Several students nodded seriously, as if meeting someone important.

My mother copied it carefully. Then *baa*. Then *taa*.

Someone behind her whispered, "If we learn fast, do you think they'll let us leave early?"

Another voice answered, "Only if we learn how to spell Saddam."

My mother did not turn around, but the corner of her mouth moved.

At home, my mother told us that the lessons were a mix of reading, writing, and arithmetic. They taught about unionism and socialism and that the Zionists were a threat to Palestine. They reminded the students about the homeland. "They want us to learn about the leaders, geography, and history of the Arab homeland."

"They never teach anything about the Chaldeans, the indigenous people of Iraq, do they?" my father asked her in a heated voice when he had taken her to class one day. "We're the native of this land, with a language so old that Jesus spoke it."

When it came to politics and religion, Babba could barely hold his tongue. My mother, on the other hand, knew how to hold hers. She kept the peace, kept silent, and waited. She was a simple woman, but very smart in her own right. She knew how to run a household large enough to resemble a small country.

My mother had three sisters and one brother, and a half brother whose mother died giving birth to him. After that, her father married again, and the house grew fuller and louder. From an early age, she learned the kinds of lessons that do not come from books: how to manage a household, how to keep peace between people who did not want it, and how to hold grief without spilling it onto others. One of her sisters, Victoria, lived in Basra. One afternoon, while cooking, her dress caught fire from the *souba*, heater. Victoria died, leaving behind three boys and a daughter. There was also the loss of George, which my mother never spoke of.

In her village, she chased the train as the British threw out gifts for the children. She was in awe at how generous they were! Her parents filled the house with love, warmth, and crops from the field, but not gifts, unless one counts the turtles or birds that her father brought home sometimes.

In the classroom, some students complained. Some attended only long enough to avoid prison. My mother attended because she always finished what she started.

She learned to write her name.

Her full name, *Shamamta*, took time and effort. It was a long name and it meant a melon in that region, a sweet summer fruit belonging to the same family as cantaloupes, cucumbers, and pumpkins.

She practiced, though, and practiced, and practiced. She wrote Sheen. Meem… Meanwhile, she heard complaints from students. One man missed a business opportunity because of the classes. Café owners said the classes turned into gossip sessions, which my mom couldn't deny. Women and men were eager to meet and talk about what this and that person did. They exchanged recipes, one telling the other that if she used this and that spice for dolma, as an example, it would be much tastier. This went on and on until the teacher begged for them to "Pay attention!"

Someone complained that the Baath Party's ideology was mixed into the lessons. Another wondered, "Why do the Bedouins get special treatments and we don't?"

"What do you mean?" asked the teacher.

"The Bedouins are assigned teachers dressed in traditional headcloth and long tunics who ride camels with their students as they go from camp to camp."

"Yeah, and sailors too," someone else said. "I heard that teachers join them during sea trips and give classes right there and then."

"I heard that truck drivers and fishermen are given taped lessons so they could study on the job," someone else said. "Why can't we get that special treatment?"

"I don't have answers to all of this," the teacher said, frustrated, "but let's pay attention to our lessons and finish lesson number one – how to write your name!"

Before she finished the rest of the letters attached to her name, my mother left Iraq with me and my younger brother. We went to Jordan, where we waited.

Later, Iraq was praised for its literacy campaign. But my mother's learning did not end there. It simply moved elsewhere.

Mamma and Babba, the day she began school.

Institute of Fine Arts Baghdad - 1971

Nine

The Old Village

⚜

"Come on," Jidu Tobia said, holding a plate of food out to us. "Eat some burghul!"

"Tobia, these are city kids," Nanna Amoona explained to him. "They don't eat burghul for breakfast."

"How about pekota?" he asked, this time offering barley instead of wheat.

"No, no, no," she said, laughing. "They don't eat burghul or pekota."

"They don't?" He asked, staring at us. Some of us had turned our noses up at his hearty breakfast offering, while others looked at him in disbelief. He's offering us a dinner entrée for breakfast? How strange!

"Then what do they eat?"

"They eat eggs, cheese, chili fry," she said as he tried to understand, clearly puzzled.

Jidu Tobia and Nanna Amoona were my mother's parents. They lived in a nice little home and were the most kind-hearted people.

After breakfast, Jidu Tobia headed to the fields, planting wheat and barley in alternating years to let the soil rest. During fallow years, he grew watermelons, cantaloupes, and cucumbers. The land of Tel Keppe sustained him, as it had sustained our people for generations.

Tel Keppe isn't where I was born, but it's where pieces of me began. We visited one summer because my grandparents, some aunts and uncles, and many cousins lived there. It was a quiet Chaldean town that felt frozen in time—the place where Mamma, Babba, and their parents were born. My father left to study and work in Baghdad, later bringing my mother there after they married.

I visited Tel Keppe only once, or so my memory tells me. The houses, without rooftops, stood side by side, their shorter walls almost touching, like friends holding hands.

Both sides of my grandparents farmed their land. Each morning, Jidu Tobia began his day at church, worked the fields all afternoon, and returned to church in the evening. After dinner, the family gathered over chai, sharing stories late into the night. No matter how busy the farm kept him, Jidu never missed his morning or evening prayers.

One day, Nanna took us through the village. As we walked, we passed the Sacred Heart Catholic Church.

"This is where your mother was baptized," she told me, proudly.

I looked at the church. I asked Nanna Amoona, "How old is this church?"

"Very, very old," she said.

"How old is that?" I asked.

"Well, it was built a few years before your mom was born," she said.

"When was my mom born?"

"In 1933."

"Oh," I said, counting in my head.

"But it's actually older than your mom," she explained. "It was built to replace an older one."

"When was the older one built?" I asked.

51

"Oh, I don't know," she said, patiently. "Almost a hundred years before that."

"What's her birthday?" I asked.

"The church?" she asked, laughing.

"No, my mom."

"It's July 1st," she answered. "But it's not her real birthday."

"It's not?"

"No. Your father is July 1st too. So is mine and Jidu's and a lot of Iraqis."

"It is?" I asked, surprised.

"Back then," she said, "no one wrote down when babies were born—especially in towns and villages. People were busy. They'd just say, 'It was spring,' or, 'Right after the harvest.'"

I frowned, trying to understand.

She smiled, lifting a hand to adjust her *qutchma*—a headdress layered with cloth and coins that rested carefully on top of her head. "But later, when the government started asking for birth dates to put on papers, they just picked one for most people who didn't know their real date. Anyone who didn't know their birthday, they picked July 1st."

"Why July 1st? That's kind of random."

She chuckled and patted my hand. "It's just an easy date to remember, right in the middle of the year."

She sighed as we passed a cemetery. "Some things don't need a date on paper to have meaning."

She led me to a large memorial at Mar Youssef (St. Joseph) Church and Shrine. It cast long shadows in the afternoon sun.

"This is where they rest," she said softly, "the forty-two girls."

Her voice carried the weight of a story I had heard whispered many times—the flood of April 1, 1949.

It was Good Friday, but nothing was good about it. That day the sky turned dark. The rain started softly, tapping on the rooftops and streets. But soon, it got louder and heavier, like a drum that wouldn't stop. Raindrops as big as miniature tennis balls fell from the heavens. The water rushed through the village, sweeping everything away. When the storm was over, it became so quiet—except for the cries of families who had lost someone. The flood took forty-four lives.

Most of the victims were young girls attending school adjacent to a church, and built on a lower floor. Among them were my Aunt Hania's daughter, just three-and-a-half years old, and her five-year-old aunt.

The young aunt had taken Hania's daughter to the Chaldean Sisters School for Girls that morning to give Hania—a pregnant mother—time to bake flatbread with their grandmother. But when the floodwater surged, my cousin and her aunt were trapped. They drowned and were later found holding hands.

I hated hearing this story. It frightened me as I imagined the scene.

The teacher, Mariam, a woman who never married, made the fateful decision to keep the children in the basement classroom, believing it would be safer. But as the floodwaters rose, the classroom turned into a trap. She told the girls to close the doors and pray, then took her nieces and went to the second floor. The older girls, nine and ten years old, managed to push their way up the stairs and survived. The younger ones, however—too small to fight against the water—drowned.

The grief that followed was unimaginable. My Aunt Hania, who helped bring me into the world years later, refused to wash her long, beautiful hair for a year after losing her daughter in the flood. She couldn't bring herself to attend her newborn son's baptism, consumed by the loss of her only girl. She took a lock of her daughter's hair, made it into a pillow, and slept on it every night for the rest of her life.

The villagers were furious, blaming the teacher for the deaths. Some even called for her execution, and one man wanted to kill her, but the people of the town stopped him. No charges were ever brought against her, because, Nanna Amoona said, "As Christians, we must forgive."

Instead, the woman lived with the guilt of her decision. "A punishment far heavier than any sentence the law might have imposed," some said while others muttered, "She probably does not care."

The tragedy was not without warning. Bishop Gamo had cautioned the villagers for years that the hill was growing weak from over-digging cemetery plots, but no one had listened. "The flood became a scar on the town," said Nanna Amoona.

Yet there were stories of survival too. My grandmother's neighbor, a clever girl attending the school that day, managed to climb onto the classroom drawers and escape through a window, pulling herself onto the roof of the building. While chaos raged below, she clung to safety, watching the waters rise and take so many lives. Some girls were lucky enough that day to be sick and not go to school.

I read out loud the names of each person on the memorial. "There's only forty-two names here," I said. "You said forty-four people died."

"Yes, there was a man and a baby, but they're buried separately," she said, and sighed. "Rumor has it that he came to his parents in a dream and asked, 'Why am I not buried with the others?'"

May they rest in peace," Nanna Amoona said with a sad voice. "Now, let's go home, *brati.*"

I loved the way she called me "daughter" in Chaldean.

As we walked back from the memorial, Nanna complimented my reading skills. "Me and your mother never went to school but we wished we had," she said. "You're going to be a reader like your father."

"Babba always walks around with a dictionary," I said.

She laughed. "That typewriter in his office, have you ever used it?"

"No," I said.

"Well, you're going to be a reader like your Babba and maybe one day you will use a typewriter too. He comes from a very learned family."

She then spoke of my grandfather, Namou, who was known as *qawasha*, meaning "the presser," because he aligned broken bones with his hands. She also spoke of my great-grandmother Maria, a legend in her time—both a powerful healer and a successful businesswoman. Maria rode horses across the northern Iraqi deserts when few women dared to do so. So loved and respected was she that one of her sons abandoned the family name Bacall and took her name instead, making Maria the family surname. In a patriarchal society, this choice caused a crack within the family.

"He was actually able to do that?" I asked.

She nodded. "Oh, others did this too," she said. "When a woman carries that much honor, her name becomes stronger than any man."

She told me that there was another Chaldean family who took the name Maria. Story had it that a woman named Maria died while she was pregnant. After she was buried, the grave keeper heard a baby crying. When he opened the grave, the child had been born and was nursing from her breasts.

I gasped, eyes wide open.

"The people called it a miracle," Nanna said. "Her family became known as *Al Lasha*, the corpse, and later as Maria."

* * *

That evening, my grandfather Tobia brought us something unexpected—a turtle.

"Take care of this turtle gently," he said, crouching down and placing the small creature in our hands. "It's a gift from the land, and it's not just a toy. Be kind to it—don't hurt it or scare it."

Watching our excitement, he added practical advice, drawn from his understanding of nature: "Keep it in the shade, not too long in the sun. The water nearby is its home, so make sure it doesn't go thirsty. And don't forget, turtles like to be quiet, just like us after a long day in the fields."

Then, with a twinkle in his eye, he reminded us of its symbolic meaning: "The turtle is patient and wise. It carries its home on its back, just like our ancestors carried their strength wherever they went. Take care of it, and it will teach you something about life—how to move slowly but surely, and how to stay strong no matter what."

At night, Jidu Tobia sat with us outside the house, watching the sun dip below the horizon. He spun his hand slowly over the land stretching around us. "Tel Keppe is in our blood," he said. "No matter where we go. The wheat, the barley, the stones—they're all part of us."

His words stayed with me as I watched him reach into the earth and pull out a clay pot, buried there to keep its contents cool. Inside was yogurt, cold as ice cream. He handed me a bowl and a plate of dates. I took a bite, savoring the taste of something so simple, and yet so extraordinary.

My grandparents in the ancestral village of Tel Keppe, later destroyed by ISIS.

Tel Keppe

My uncle at the farm.

Ten

The Unfinished House

One night, when my sister Niran was twelve, the Virgin Mary came to her. She wore a long blue robe and floated in front of Niran, as light as a butterfly.

This was it—Niran's chance to ask for something big, something that could save us all. Rumor had it that if the Virgin Mary appears in your dream, she'll grant you any wish. Niran knew exactly what to wish for: "Save our house," she wanted to say. Every day, she heard our parents whisper and cry about losing the house.

But when Niran opened her mouth, no words came out. Her voice was stuck in her throat. She tried again. Nothing.

The Virgin Mary waited, her soft gaze full of patience. Niran tried to crawl toward her, desperate to make the words come out. But the Virgin started floating farther and farther away, like a bird disappearing into the sky. And then she was gone.

When Niran woke up, she cried. She felt like she had failed us all.

Back then, we lived in the neighborhood I mentioned earlier—Al Sikak, the Railway District. I've already told you what it looked like: how close it was to the station, how carefully it was kept. It was, by every measure, perfect. Our house had gardens in the front and back. There was a movie theater nearby and a private club where my siblings went swimming. Guards stood at every corner, and the streets felt very safe.

Because my father worked for the railway, keeping track of the books, the government gave us the house to rent for almost nothing—a single dinar a month. Then, in 1968, Iraq's new president, Ahmad Hassan Al Bakr, made an offer to government workers. He gave them free land in Al Sikak to build houses on, plus loans to get started. My father took the deal and started building a big, two-story house.

At the time, there were eleven of us kids, plus our parents. My two married sisters were supposed to live upstairs with their husbands and kids, while the rest of us stayed downstairs. The house was going to be a fresh start for all of us.

But building a house in Iraq wasn't easy. My father ran out of money before it was finished. All it still needed was plumbing, electricity, and tiles. He asked his brother and sisters to lend him 1,000 dinars to complete it, a small amount at the time, one that would not have changed their lives. But they said no. One of our aunts told the others it was his fault for trusting the wrong person, a man related to us, who had taken the money meant for the house. The hard details of that story are for another time. My father trusted him because he was family, and because he believed family looked after one another. It was a mistake, one that my mother and the children paid for too.

Without the loan, my father couldn't finish the house. Then a man at his job, the same one who had sent him to work in a faraway city, told him he had to give the rental house back to the government. Babba refused to leave. He had nine children waiting for him at home.

Niran, still feeling guilty about her dream, decided to do something bold. She asked her school friend Hayfa for help. Hayfa wasn't just any friend—she was the daughter of Iraq's president.

In those years, schools often reflected where families lived. The best private and state schools were in neighborhoods like Al Karkh and Al Mansur, where ministers, government officials, wealthy merchants, and foreign diplomats had their homes. Back then, even presidential families lived in regular houses by today's standards, close enough that their children went to school with children like us.

Hayfa and Niran shared a desk at school. Hayfa was kind, pretty, and a little spoiled. Every day, she brought a lunchbox full of treats and always let Niran take the first sip of her Pepsi. When Hayfa arrived late to class, she'd sit wherever she wanted, even if it meant moving someone else. Teachers never said a word to her.

One day, Niran finally worked up the courage to tell Hayfa about our troubles. "Can your father help us keep the house?" she asked.

Hayfa looked sad. "I don't even see my father," she said. "When he comes home, I'm already asleep."

That was the end of that.

They turned off our electricity. They turned off our water.

It was winter. At night, candles burned low, their wax dripping onto saucers. During midterm exams, my three older sisters went to stay with our great-uncle so they could study under real light. The rest of us, including Heyam, a sister in fifth grade, stayed behind. When the water was gone, my mother waited until evening and sent her to the neighbor with a hose. We washed clothes and boiled water quickly, before anyone complained. Eventually, they did.

The neighbors spoke to the authorities. The hose disappeared. Without light or water, everything became harder. Heyam failed fifth grade. In those years, you had to pass every class to move on. She had to repeat the year.

In the end, my father couldn't save the house. We lost the rental, too, and had to move to a rough neighborhood in Al-Salihiya where the kids threw rocks at our windows for fun and stared at us with open hatred. My father tried to sell some land he owned in the north, but even that didn't work. The deeds were with the same aunt who refused to lend him money. Each time he asked for them, she claimed she couldn't find them. Years later, she gave them to another relative, as if they were hers to decide.

We lost everything. The house. The rental. The land. And when Saddam Hussein later announced that anyone living in a government rental could keep it for free, it was too late for us. Another opportunity gone.

Not long after, we moved again, into a *mujtamel*—a small added room attached to my aunt's house. Things began to improve, slightly.

Basim and a friend, waiting.

63

Eleven

Basim's Dream

Basim, my oldest brother, watched the newspaper vendor near our house. He watched with longing. He wanted to read the daily paper, and to do so daily. But he could not afford it, not daily. How could he read the paper without paying for it or stealing it? An idea came to him.

He walked to the vendor and said, "I don't have the full price, but let me pay half. I'll sit here and read the paper, then return it, and you'll still make money."

The vendor laughed but agreed, and at thirteen years old, Basim became a familiar face at the newsstand. He would stand or sit there for hours, the papers rustling in his hands as he read headlines about distant countries, coups, and revolutions.

The more he read, the more he felt like an outsider in his own country. Growing up as a Christian in Iraq meant living on the fringes of a society where you were tolerated but never truly accepted. Even as a child, he knew there was no future for him there. By the time he was in sixth grade, he had made up his mind: *I am leaving this country. I don't know when or how, but I will leave.*

He didn't even hide his indifference toward school. "Why should I care about grades?" he would tell anyone who asked. "I'm not staying here."

His teachers scolded him, and his mother worried about his lack of interest in his studies. But Basim didn't care. He spent his time devouring newspapers instead, learning everything he could about the world beyond Iraq.

"I hate the Baath Party," he told Babba. "I hated the Nasserists before them too. One is worse than the other. They all discriminated against Christians, and under Saddam, it didn't matter who you were—Christian, Muslim, anyone. They discriminated against humanity itself."

My dad listened to and agreed with him, but my mom begged him to stay away from politics. But the political atmosphere in Iraq only cemented his resolve to leave. Arrests, disappearances, and executions were common. The streets felt heavy with fear, like dark clouds gathering before a storm. That made Basim be always careful about whom he associated with. If a friend became a Baathist, he cut him off immediately.

Basim constantly argued with Babba. "You're too kind," he told Babba. "You trust people who don't deserve it and gave too much of yourself. That's why they always take advantage of you."

Babba didn't listen. He always hoped for the best in people. Basim's frustration with him grew as he got older. He saw how others manipulated his father's good nature, promising to help him build a house, yes, *thee* house, only to abandon him once the money ran out. "Don't trust them," he begged. "They're liars. They'll leave you with nothing."

But Babba didn't listen. The family's financial struggles weighed heavily on Basim. He dreamed of a life where they didn't have to rely on others, where they could stand on their own. He knew that life wouldn't happen in Iraq. He knew he had to risk it all.

At eighteen, Basim attempted to leave Iraq. Babba cried the day he left. "I don't want you to go," he said. "I don't know what will happen to you there."

"I have to go, Babba. There's no future for me or our family here."

Basim traveled to Bulgaria, hoping to find a way to build a new life. But the experience was humbling. A teacher there encouraged him to return to Iraq and finish high school. Although that wasn't what he wanted to do, that was what he did. He went back. He finished school, but he knew it was only temporary."

Returning to Iraq simply deepened his resolve to leave. By then, the government had tightened its control over everything, including the oil industry. The Baath Party's rise to power in 1968 had turned Iraq into a place of paranoia and repression. There was no rest, no security, no freedom.

He managed to avoid military service by enrolling in college, but his mind was always elsewhere. He dreamed of America.

Basim's determination to leave was met with skepticism by some in the family. His aunt's husband once told him, "You think it's easy to get to America?"

"I don't care where I go as long as it's not Iraq," Basim said.

"Why do you want to leave so badly?" the uncle persisted. "Wherever you go, life is the same."

Basim shook his head. "No," he replied. "There's a life where you know what will happen tomorrow, and there's a life where you don't. There's a life with democracy and freedom, and there's a life without it. They're not the same."

"Son, you don't know what you're talking about," the uncle continued.

"I do know," said Basim. "I know I have no future in Iraq. I have to leave, not just for myself, but for the family. I want everyone to have a chance at a better life."

He saved every dinar he could, constantly looking for an opportunity to escape. His father, though reluctant at first, began to support him, giving him money whenever he needed it. Everyone watched and waited for the right moment. When that moment came, Basim left.

He was the first to leave Iraq, but he never meant to be the only one. What he carried with him was more than his own hope. It was the belief that one day, we would all be together again, somewhere new.

Basim reads a newspaper

Basim leaves Iraq

About the Author

I was born in Baghdad, Iraq, into a Chaldean Christian family, and grew up in an Aramaic-speaking home—the language Jesus spoke. When I was ten years old, my family immigrated to Michigan, carrying with us memories, language, and stories that would shape my life.

I am known as the Chaldean Storyteller and have written dozens of books and produced award-winning films. Through my work, I return to the places and voices of my childhood, preserving stories of identity, memory, and belonging.

To learn more, visit https://weamnamou.com/

Also by Weam Namou

_∽◦◦◦∽_

Weam Namou has written across many genres, including memoir, nonfiction, fiction, and poetry. In recent years, she has turned her focus to Young Adult literature, where she is best known for her _Magical Museum_ series. _The Chaldean Storyteller_ series is her most recent work.

The Magical Museum: Mesopotamian Mania
When a group of sixth graders visits the Chaldean Museum, history comes alive. In the Ancient Mesopotamia Gallery, mosaic lions roar, cuneiform tablets whisper secrets, and the towering Code of Hammurabi holds a mysterious power. As the past awakens around them, the students discover that history isn't just something you study—it's something you experience.

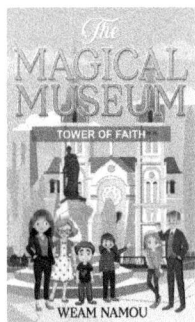

The Magical Museum: Tower of Faith
What secrets lie hidden in the Faith and Church Gallery of the Chaldean Museum? When a group of sixth graders steps inside, they discover it is far more than an exhibit—it is a gateway into the enduring story of the Chaldean people. As questions echo through the gallery and artifacts stir to life, the students are drawn toward a symbolic tower that stands for faith, resilience, and survival.

The Magical Museum: Village Whispers

Step into the Village Life Gallery, where the voices of Chaldean villages still echo. As a group of sixth graders explores scenes from northern Iraq's ancient towns, lantern-lit homes, church bells, and familiar traditions bring the past to life. In places like Tel Keppe and Alqosh, the students discover a legacy of faith, family, and resilience—one that continues to shape generations.

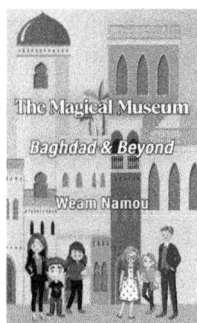

The Magical Museum: Baghdad & Beyond

What stories await in the Baghdad & Beyond Gallery? As a group of sixth graders steps into Baghdad's crowded streets, date-palm courtyards, and book-lined cafés along the Tigris, the city's rhythm comes alive. Copper workshops ring with sound, oud melodies drift through the air, and family gatherings reveal the creativity and resilience of the Chaldean people—connecting Baghdad's past to the lives still shaped by it today.

www.ingramcontent.com/pod-product-compliance
Lightning Source LLC
Chambersburg PA
CBHW032051040426
42449CB00007B/1067